Our Words Are Powerful

We Are Here For A Reason

Words To Power

Our Words Are Powerful: We Are Here For A Reason

This book is a publication of

Copyright © 2022 by Words To Power

All rights reserved. No part of this book may be reproduced or transmitted in any form or by any means without written permission of the author.

To the youth finding their purpose and passion.
You are here for a reason!

Acknowledgments

Thank you to the young poets who shared their powerful words in this book. Special thank you to the numerous schools that provided us the opportunity and privilege to present our spoken word poetry workshops for your students during the 2021-2022 school year. We look forward to continuing those partnerships. We greatly appreciate the Caring for Denver Foundation, Rose Community Foundation, and the City of Denver for providing the funding necessary to publish, celebrate, and distribute books of poetry written by underserved youth as part of our school-based programs (workshops and open mic events), all to encourage creative expression that reduces isolation, increases self-confidence, and increases the use of poetry and spoken word for coping and resilience.

Foreword

Welcome to "Our Words Are Powerful," a yearly youth-written book of poetry from the Denver area edited, published, and distributed by Words To Power. With the theme of "The Struggle Is Real So Is Our Resilience," the 2021 book was an incredible success. For 2022, we were able to inspire almost twice the number of submissions with the theme "We Are Here For A Reason." With that focus and through Words To Power poetry workshops, we wanted to guide youth in finding and pursuing their purpose with determination. As you will read, these young people exceeded our expectations. We hope their powerful words inspire you just as much as they did for us.

For those who do not know about our organization: Words To Power conducts highly engaging and culturally relevant spoken word poetry workshops for Brown and other underserved youth in elementary, middle, and high schools in the Denver metro area and throughout Colorado. We partner with schools to produce poetry events with multiple participating classes coming together to share their spoken word with each other. Words To Power publishes a yearly youth-written poetry book, with most submissions coming from our workshop participants. We host a book release event with contributors reading their poetry for their families and the greater community. Words To Power collaboratively organizes quarterly community open mic events featuring youth who consistently participate in our programs.

The Words To Power logo draws inspiration from many sources. The overall structure is modeled after a corn plant, as our workshop curriculum uses it as a metaphor. The raised fist reminds us of our power to create change, as social justice movements before us have struggled to achieve. The scrolls on either side pull from Indigenous books in Mexico, as symbols of speech (thus the accompanying image from a codex of people talking to each other). Taken together, our words and power come from our roots.

Table of Contents

Instruments in the Forest at Day and Night by Angelo R. Martinez Rangel (age 10) 1

What Does Black Mean to Me? by Kendal C. Hill (age 10) 2

Mi Cultura by Paola (age 10) 3

One Day by Giovanny Soto (age 11) 4

Life Can and Will Change by Eyan (age 11) 5

Takeover by Aianna Bruce (age 11) 6

I Can Change The World by Yadira Lopez (age 11) 8

With Our Voices by Charley Peter Stiles (age 11) 9

You Matter by Saith Robles (age 11) 10

Rain by Lexi (age 12) 11

Fighters by Raul (age 12) 12

We Are Powerful by Natalia Rodriguez (age 12) 13

Our World by Joslynn (age 12) 14

Why Are We Here by Forest Jean Reed (age 12) 16

A Person by Izaak Grossetete (age 12) 17

Fire of Life by Adrian (age 12) 18

Underneath Boxes by Nelli (age 12) 19

Light in Darkness by Jelani Lozano (age 12) 20

Together We Are Powerful by Jelani Lozano (age 12) 21

My Soccer Life by Jayr (age 13) 22

True Meaning Behind Rap by Joshua Martinez (age 14) 23

Break Free by Joshua Martinez (age 14) 24

You Have Taken My Name by Estrella Acosta-Alire (age 14) 26

Love Letter to Our Lord by Gina Alfaro (age 14) 28

Do Not Be Afraid by Jayleene Muniz Lozano (age 14) 30

Skating Dream by Samuel (age 15) 31

I Am by Tanera Dotson (age 15) 32

Trust by Analeese Lomeli (age 15) 34

My Beautiful Butterfly by Analeese Lomeli (age 15) 35

Algos by Rowan Lopez (age 15) 36

The American Dream by Journie (age 15) 38

Anxiety by Carlos (age 15) 39

This Chain Keeps Me Sane by Carlos (age 15) 40

Still Here by Autumn (age 15) 41

The Rainbow Within the Storm by Autumn (age 15) 44

Survivor by Karen "Jazhubi" Salgado (age 15) 45

Little Did She Know by Rosalyn Leyba (age 15) 47

The Path by Jeremiah Espinoza (age 16) 49

Focused by Jeremiah Espinoza (age 16) 50

Times Up by Brylynn Hurtado (age 17) 51

Golden Butterfly by Yumna Ali (age 17) 54

Let Your Life Speak by Cydney Brown (age 18) 55

Black Girl by Cydney Brown (age 18) 57

Unknown by Amari (age 18) 60

Mirrors by Amari (age 18) 61

The Universe Took Its Time With You by Aakanksha Adya (age 18) 64

Pro Black by Tracie Taylor (age 21) 65

I Choose to Rise by Evelyn Neal (age 21) 66

Dear Black Men by Evelyn Neal (age 21) 68

Instruments in the Forest at Day and Night by Angelo R. Martinez Rangel (age 10)

(inspired by "Peter and the Wolf")

The sun sings as it shines in the forest.
The piano makes a tune at the river.
The hand moves like water
sliding across the river,
hitting the rocks
as if they are keys.
Water splashes turn into musical notes.
The bird chirps like a flute.
The woodpecker sounds like a snare drum.
The ducks sound like a clarinet.
The moon sings when the sun goes to sleep.
The fireflies light up like a disco ball.
The piano keeps on playing the same tune
but with different animals.
The owl sings like a whistle.
Frogs burp like a bass drum.
The wolf howls like a horn.
The piano always plays,
no matter the day.

What Does Black Mean to Me? by Kendal C. Hill (age 10)

Black is shades.
Black is beauty.
Black is history.

What Does Black Mean?

Black is growth.
Black is strength.
Black is peace.

What Does Black Mean?

Black is then.
Black is now.
Black is forever.

Black is you and me
growing
and coming together

Mi Cultura by Paola (age 10)

Yo soy un sol.
Yo soy historia
en el futuro.
Ellos creen que soy nada,
pero la verdad
yo soy muchas cosas.
Vengo de El Salvador
y de mi creador.
Yo soy las pupusas que mi mamá hace.
Ellos me comen con tenedor,
tratando de cambiar mi cultura.
En el espejo,
veo mi cultura,
y veo un brillante día
en mi corazón.
En mis sueños
imagino que me respeten
y que no me juzguen por mi cultura.
Con nuestras voces,
podemos hablar
y cambiar nuestro futuro.
En nuestras manos,
podemos hacer historia.
Juntos,
podemos cambiar el mundo.
Somos todos los mismos y únicos.

One Day by Giovanny Soto (age 11)

I am a kid
who wants the world
to be a better place.
Soon,
I will wake up one day
to a new world
where everything
is a good place
and not a bad place

Life Can and Will Change by Eyan (age 11)

I come from my mother's soul
and extremely intelligent ancestors.
When I look in the mirror,
I see greatness,
power,
the next Martin Luther King Jr.
With all our voices,
together we can change what is wrong
and make it right.
In our hands,
we hold power.
Sometimes people do not have a lot,
so we work with what we have.
My family was always feeling down
when they were younger
because they could not move on with life
without papers.
They stood up
and said no,
we do not need some papers
to tell us what we can
and cannot do.
Just because I am different
does not mean I need papeles
to succeed
and make changes.
They are my inspiration
to keep me going.
That is why
together,
we stand to make a difference.
We are,
and always will be,
the Globeville commUNITY
and we stand strong.

Takeover by Aianna Bruce (age 11)

We are a beautiful Black culture
fighting for our rights.
We should still have time
to fight for our rights.
All people should still
be able to stay alive.
Cops pull us over,
shoot,
then we die.
Our families cry,
hoping we are still alive.
I cannot get some chips
because they told me
I was too dark.
I might steal
and my mom is the driver
in the runaway car.
I wanted to say thank you,
this motivates us.
I get dirty looks
walking to school sometimes.
It feels like it comes from nature too.
But sometimes I just laugh
knowing what I can do.
When I go on fox news,
I see all this negative stuff.
It does hurt me a lot.
But I know we can change it.
We still have time
and we are going to use it.
It is time to take over.

On December 18, 1865,
that was when we started to know
what we could do
to stop picking cotton
and stop getting beat.

And we did it.
So,
we can stop all of it
by using words
and body movements.
We carry strength,
intelligence,
and most of all teamwork.
It is time to take over.

I Can Change The World by Yadira Lopez (age 11)

I am a Salvadorian
who wants to make my parents proud,
like Simba following his dad's footsteps.
I come from the most beautiful place ever known.
It shines like the raging sun on a hot day.
When I look in the mirror,
I see a beautiful young girl
getting ready for a change in her life,
like a caterpillar turning into a butterfly.
In my dreams,
I imagine myself making a change in the world
by helping homeless people get a job
and get a house
with clouds on the ceiling
and rainbows in the dawn of light,
just to start over in life.

With Our Voices by Charley Peter Stiles (age 11)

With our voices,
we can say what we believe.
We can be what we want to be.
Using our hands,
we can make a fist
and choose to fight back.
We all have flags of different colors.
Be what you want to be,
become what you want to become.
No one can tell you
who to be
or what to do.
We can stand tall
and overcome all our fears.
Even though it might sting
to be called a slur,
know you are more than an insult.
Everyone can have a change in their hearts.
You can choose to stand.
We know that we can stand up for our rights.

You Matter by Saith Robles (age 11)

My life
is like a roller coaster.
There are ups and downs,
twists and turns.
But being with someone
you trust and care about
can really help.
When you feel like you do not matter,
they are there for you
ready to pick you up.
But you do not need someone
to know you matter
or to know you are perfect
the way you are.
If your life is like a roller coaster,
just know:
there is always someone there with you.
That person is you.

Rain by Lexi (age 12)

I am you.
I come from your mind.
I talk to you
when nobody wants to.
You hear me tapping on the window
when it is gloomy outside,
like a foggy swamp.
There are no frogs,
or fish,
or anything really.
But there is rain.

Fighters by Raul (age 12)

We are fighters
but we may not always fight together.
We may fight against each other
but friendship will always overpower fights.
We will fight for respect
and will never give up.
We will always carry people
who failed to earn respect
by holding people up
and bringing them together.

We Are Powerful by Natalia Rodriguez (age 12)

Con nuestras voces,
we can fix this world
and make it a little better.
In our hands,
we hold the power to accomplish this.
We also hold a future for our families,
the people we love,
and ourselves.
We each decide
whether that future will be good
or bad.
Together,
we should strive
to make the miserable parts
of this world
better.
En este mundo,
there are a lot of people
with problems.
After all,
we are all human.
So,
why should it be so difficult
to help each other?
We are human.
We all have dream
and together,
we are all
very,
very powerful.

Our World by Joslynn (age 12)

I am my family's pride and joy.
I come from a world
with discrimination and racism,
all because we do not look the same.
When I look in the mirror,
I see my difference,
my uniqueness.
It is who I am
and I am proud of it.
In my dreams,
I imagine a world,
a world where everyone
would be treated the same,
where everyone would get along
and there would be no racism
just because of our skin.
With our voices,
we could rise high,
raise our voices
to defend ourselves,
because it is us
and only us
they would hear.
In our hands,
we have the power
to change the way
others are viewed
and change the wrong
to the right.
Together,
we rise high
to prove our point.
We are all beautiful
and unique
in our own ways.
We love ourselves
because it is us.
We are all humans.

We all have feelings
and voices.
None of us are the exact same,
We do not talk
or speak the same.
Never be ashamed.

Why Are We Here by Forest Jean Reed (age 12)

Why are we here?
A question that everyone asks in fear.
We know there is a reason.
We are here
to fight for the future.
But what power do we have
over what we will not be here for?
Why are we here?
If older generations knew what was fair
maybe us kids
would say they care.
We are what the future will be.
We are here for a reason,
because we are the key.
Why are we here?
We might not feel it
but we are prepared
to fight for what the world
has in store.
Our eyes sting with tears
and our muscles are sore.
But we will still shout for our rights.
We will try to win more.
We will try to win this fight
and we will be the light.
Why are we here?
No one should ever have to live
in fear.
Our words will linger,
our legacy will stay,
until humankind sheds a final tear

A Person by Izaak Grossetete (age 12)

I am a person,
an entity.
I come from my mother,
my father,
brothers,
and sisters.
When I look in the mirror,
I see all of them,
all of them in me,
all my ancestors
who shaped me,
and came before me.
With our voices,
we can build,
we can destroy,
we can create
and relate,
or we can obliterate
and control.
In our hands,
we hold the power,
the power to do
and to be.
Together,
we can build a better future,
for us and for them.
We are in this together
for you,
and for me.

Fire of Life by Adrian (age 12)

My life is like a fire,
it keeps going.
With the wood you put in,
it grows bigger and stronger,
just like my family's courage
makes me bigger and stronger.
Fire has its limits,
just like us.
Fire is a living thing
and so are we.
Fire has an end.
Everyone has an end to life as well.

Underneath Boxes by Nelli (age 12)

People always tell me:
"Follow your dreams."
"Choose the right path."
"Do not leave what you want
behind closed doors
underneath boxes in a closet."
Someone will always tell you,
"Do something better
because I do not think
that is good."
With all the weight
building up on your shoulders,
let it go.
The time is now.
Do not watch the clock.
Ignore the whispers
telling you what would happen
and what would you do,
because it is good
if it feels right to you.

Light in Darkness by Jelani Lozano (age 12)

There is always some kind of light
in the darkness.
That light can lead you somewhere great.
Although you might crisscross directions,
you can still make it to your destination.
Negativity can always be turned into positivity
with the changes you make.
If you try,
you can accomplish anything.
You are worth it
and you can make a change.

Together We Are Powerful by Jelani Lozano (age 12)

She spread her wings
and soared high.
He made a change in the community
and inspired them.
They continued to help the environment,
until everyone was successful.
They showed their power
and continued to soar high
into the sky
becoming even more powerful.
They fought together.
Inspiration touched everyone.
Continuing to become stronger,
they made a change.
They planted a seed
that continued to grow.

My Soccer Life by Jayr (age 13)

My life
is like soccer.
When someone
tries to take the ball
away from me,
it feels like an obstacle
I experienced
when I got hurt.
But I faced it.
I want to accomplish great things:
high school,
college,
becoming a doctor.
When the other team slides
to get the ball,
it feels like someone
trying to take something important
from you:
mom,
dad,
siblings,
cousins,
house,
dogs.
When the ball goes out,
you can lose things in your life.
With the throw in
or corner kick,
they will come back.
If you want to accomplish your goals,
you need to work together
with your family
as your soccer team.

True Meaning Behind Rap by Joshua Martinez (age 14)

The true meaning of rap
is not what some people think.
Some think it is music
or just someone singing.
There are some
who see passed the beat of the song
or the singer singing his or her lyrics.
They see and hear the story behind it,
what the song is truly about,
the singer's story.
You just need to listen carefully
to see the story
that is being told to you.
So next time
you hear a rap song you like,
you should try to find out the story
to see what the rapper
is trying to tell you.
They could be trying to tell you
how difficult their life was,
what life was like for them
when they were children,
what they did in school,
how they started to sing,
or what motivates them.
So next time
you listen to a rap song,
try and find their story
to better understand
the true meaning of the music
and why they made the song.
You can then
better understand them
and their story.

Break Free by Joshua Martinez (age 14)

I am a man
who has risen
from his parents'
hopes and dreams
for a better future,
a future that I will help create
with the building blocks of success.
But I cannot do it all
without the help from my community.
First,
they need to stop being a bag of potatoes,
going where people want them to go
and doing what people tell them to do.
They must break free from man's grip
to carve the path they choose,
not the path made for them.

To break free,
they need
to want
to be successful,
they must try to be successful.
It starts with one thing:
a dream.
I dream of the wondrous things
that my community and I
will do.
But that is
all it is,
a dream
that soon
can become a reality.
But first,
we,
as the people of this world,
must break free
for our dreams
to become a reality.

Together,
we can move mountains
and build buildings
so advanced
that they would change our lives.
But first,
we must break free.
We must grow our wings
of courage and success.
We will build our future
for us,
our people.
Then,
we must teach
our next generation
to break free,
so they can teach
the next generation,
all the way down
to the ends of the world,
until
we no longer need
to break free.

You Have Taken My Name by Estrella Acosta-Alire (age 14)

You have taken my name.
Hear me.
Can you not hear our screams
as a result of your oppressive means,
being suppressed by our own country's schemes?
We get dirt for work
because of our dreams
and need for some cash.
Treated as lower-class,
my people are thrown in the trash.

You have taken my name.
See me.
Mi cultura y la evidencia
lay before your eyes.
You can hear the beautiful,
brown people's cries.
Our children are trapped
and you try to disguise
the culture and blood
we attempt to pass down to our kin.
But how can we,
when they are locked behind bars
due to your sin?

You have taken my name.
Deceive me.
Becoming a forgotten race,
our problems are overlooked,
not a trace.
The fights we have fought
for our rights to this land,
our education and political rights
being crushed by your hand.
We must stand,
as a gate around our heritage
and dignity,
for who I am.

You have taken my name.
Leave me,
sitting still
watching you
colonize who we are,
killing us
with pesticides and arms.
You make us pick up your mess
being left behind
as you pick up a new protest.
Here for five hundred years,
yet still going unnoticed.

You have taken my name.
Teach me.
Give me the education
my parents fought for,
had to pry the doors open to college
years before.
Let me know how to say my name,
to believe your history
and everything you proclaim.

You have taken my name.
Endear me.
A-stray me from mis sueños
and las estrellas that I see in the sky.
A-coast I will drift,
far from who I am
and watch as my people cry.
A-liar,
I will be called,
when telling los cuentos
that have been passed on.
Mi nombre es
Estrella Luz Citlauia Acosta-Alire
No seré suprimido por tu orgullo.

Love Letter to Our Lord by Gina Alfaro (age 14)

Inside of me
is a piece of my creator,
for I am his creation.
When he is with me,
nothing can stand in my way.
A mishap can happen
but you are there to heal me.
Your voice gives me peace of mind.
You let me off the hook
so many times.

I fail to fulfill you
and your destiny.
I want to be there for you
but then I get bored.
How can I demand a fulltime father
when I am sometimes a halftime daughter?
I have been baptized in your waters.
I was given your piece of bread
and cup of wine.
I have been freed
from the greatest punishments.

I am your disciple,
but continuously I fall from you.
I pollute myself with violence,
lies,
and then I go and silence your voice.
I prefer your kingdom
but prefer the expiring earthly choices.
But what is more important?
Your fruits.
But even with your fruits,
it is a constant battle.

Many do not understand sin.
People think you are a strict
and pompous God,

but you know the harm it does.
Many also think you are a God of hate
and then they hate and slander you
without even reading what you have done
and what you have taught.

As one of the many brown daughters you have made,
my brothers and sisters chose to deny and ignore you
because of colonization.
The funny thing is,
you have never been a gospel of hate.
People who are in the branch of LGBTQ+
do not even get a chance to meet you
because the homophobic representatives in church.
What sucks in the end
is that people become so scared
to even embrace or invite you in
because of what some followers choose to do.
I would love it
if people would give you a second chance
and let go of the trauma.

Besides that,
no matter what we do,
you love us so much
and give us many chances
even when we become entangled
with the earthly and flesh romances.
We look for something to cling to,
a deeper meaning to life
or something fulfilling.
With you,
whether or not I have love
from somebody else,
I have you.
And who can love like you do,
no one.
No one but you Jesus.

Do Not Be Afraid by Jayleene Muniz Lozano (age 14)

Do not be afraid
to try new things
just because you care about
what other people think.
People can try to tell you
who you are
but it is up to you to ignore them
and make it far.
Keep your eyes
on the red target,
it will be your ticket
to the future.
Trying new things gives you ideas
of who you want to be
so do not feel lost and stuck
in the deep sea.
Life can be hard
and make you nervous
but it is time
to find your purpose.
Life is much more
than trying to impress.
Just be yourself,
do not hide under a dress.

Skating Dream by Samuel (age 15)

I skate.
These wheels
are my escape.
I pray
they take me away.
I feel the wind
blow across my face,
feeling so free.
This is my escape.

I Am by Tanera Dotson (age 15)

I am a positive person,
unaffected by negativity.
I wonder,
where is all the love in the world?
Why is there so much negativity?
How do we fix this?
Are we ready to take action?
I see killing in this world,
hate,
and people scared
to just take a walk in the park.
I want to see love in this world.
I want to see hope,
peace,
and people hugging
instead of fighting.
I want to see people
motivate one another.
How do we fix this?
Are you ready to take action?
I am a positive person,
unaffected by negativity.
I pretend
to be happy in this world.
I pretend
to be a different person.
I touch the people I love
to remind myself
of all the love in the world,
the positivity.
I worry about our new generation
having to be raised in this crazy world.
How do we fix this?
Am I ready to take action?
I cry,
thinking about all the families
who have lost their loved ones.
I am a positive person,

unaffected by negativity.
I understand there is love and hate
and we all need to come together
and be equal.
How do I fix this?
I am ready to take action.
I say that there is hope,
peace,
faith,
and love in the world.
I dream that one day,
we all can come together as equals.
I dream that we can stop the violence

Trust by Analeese Lomeli (age 15)

Trust,
protect it.
Trust,
be careful who you give it to
because it will not always come back
the same way.
It can break
and leave you with scars.
It can be the one thing
people just give out,
like pieces of candy.
Trust,
with it
comes loyalty.
Trust,
once you give it to someone,
they always have choices.
They can throw it on the ground
and just let you watch it shatter
or they can protect it
with all they have inside of them.
But,
so do you.
You see,
it works both ways,
like teamwork.
You need to make sure
the person you are trusting,
is trusting you too.

My Beautiful Butterfly by Analeese Lomeli (age 15)

I see the beauty in your being,
as you fly around me,
flapping your colorful wings.
I know it is you abuela.
I feel it is you.
You are free now,
no more hurting,
no more pain.
As I see you fly around
in your beautiful colors,
I feel a tear
falling from down my cheek.
But it is not one of sadness,
nor anger,
nor pain,
but joy
and love.
My beautiful butterfly.

Algos by Rowan Lopez (age 15)

The beauty of the pain,
the beauty many hate,
but a great amount that agree and confide
in this beautiful beast.

The beast of pain
is the snake
that tempted Adam and Eve,
the cheese that trapped the mouse,
and the curiosity that killed the cat.

The beast that brought upon demise,
flooded its victims in iron of its own being
and themselves.

Its victims breathe the iron
as if they have been holding their breath
for hours on end,
indulge in it
as if it is water in a drought,
relishing the iron
like it was the victim's favorite sweet,
and savoring it like a steak.

I am the beast.
My claws are merely
an extension of my being.
My sharp blades were made for the purpose
of bringing something into this world,
adding beauty into this world.

The sharp blade,
its handle engraved
with beautiful markings,
the jewel that comes from the handle,
the blade,
its acute edges,
the iron that comes from the Earth

meeting the Earth's own creation.
This idolized jewel that I keep
like a millionaire in his collection.
Only,
I am different.
I truly appreciate this jewel that I keep.

I am the artist,
the beast
that holds this beautifully engraved handle,
with the jewel on the handle.
It is an art tool that the beast-
that I use
cutting and slashing its-
my empty canvas.

The canvas that the Earth has given me,
the canvas my mother has given me,
the canvas my family has raised
and see grown into an empty canvas
that they love for a reason
that I do not have a sense in knowing.

The beast's canvas-
my canvas the thing that I see day after day,
shower after shower,
dressing after dressing,
and slashing after carving.

I am the beast.
I am the beauty in the pain.
I am the artist,
and I am the fool,
the fool that has fallen in love
with the beast,
which is me,
like a sailor
who has fallen in love with a siren.

The American Dream by Journie (age 15)

No child should be afraid
to go to school
and on the way,
wonder
if they will die that day.
Lockdown drills
should not even exist.
We go to learn.
Why is our life at risk?
Everyone is shocked on the news,
but in America,
guns are too precious to lose.
Do not prioritize power
over lives,
instead,
protect people,
children,
who do not deserve to die.

Anxiety by Carlos (age 15)

They say take a breath.
I try,
but every gasp
feels like I am getting stabbed in the chest.
The words that come out of my mouth
sound like gibberish.
I just think,
is this it,
is this the end?
Meanwhile,
my vision goes completely red.
My emotions fly everywhere.
But it is okay though,
because it does not take long
for me to gain back control.
That is not what I worry about.
All these eyes are on me
like I am the only thing that stands out.
It would feel better
if you put your hand out,
but that is not the case.
What happens is
I get it thrown in my face,
like I am supposed to be the big serious man
who sits around
and gets made fun of
and does not take a stand.
This feeling in my chest
is not one I could easily put to rest.
But I know every single day is a test
to see if I can deal with people
and emotions
and give it my best.

This Chain Keeps Me Sane by Carlos (age 15)

This chain keeps me sane
when the things I go through
cause a strain.
Every day I wake up,
I feel the thin strap of steel
that makes the pain fade.
The bullet that holds my uncle
reminds me of all the times we chuckled.
The cold steel against my chest
puts all my dark emotions to rest.
If I did not have this chain,
I do not think I would be the same.
This chain keeps me sane.

Still Here by Autumn (age 15)

I am frybread.
I am the striking fragrance
that catches your nose,
the happiness
that fills you
when smelling it.
I will never forget
the sweat dripping down
my grandma's forehead,
breathing in exhaust,
flushed skin from carrying traditions,
traditions of food and culture,
lost traditions.
So as frybread is being made,
takoja's of the new generation
are patiently waiting
for the sound of Unci's voice
to tell them it is done,
telling them it is time to listen,
to listen to the traditions,
the stories,
the memories,
memories of South Dakota,
Youth strikes upon your soul,
the hot air breathing on your neck,
just like the warm embrace
of grandma's arms around you.
The wind dances and ruffles through your hair,
just like grandma's comb,
preparing your hair to be braided.
You remember the cold,
chilling your skin at night,
just like the ice-cold touch of grandma's hands.
My grandma:
the foundation of our tree,
her roots bind us like leather.
I see myself
within the reflection in my grandma's soul.

The careful creases in her face,
formed by worn down fat and tissue,
are still beautiful nonetheless.
The delicacy of her hands
sew past, present, and future
into the hem of the fabric,
the fabric that now holds the embers of the fire
burned by our ancestors,
That fabric now holds the beauty
our ancestors felt when celebrating.
we feel this chariot that is time,
catch up to us minute by minute.
We feel the pride and power
bleed into us,
feeling the silk of this traveled fabric
attach to your skin,
just as the genocide of your people
has attached to your existence.
The black sky absorbs your eyes,
just like those memories absorb your mind.
You look at the stars,
seeing your ancestors watch over you.
They watch over you
and see
the loss,
the heartbreak,
the joy,
and the happiness
that your family has experienced.
You,
as in
me,
we,
and I.
These images flash in my mind
as I look at the sky.
You feel the guilt of this world
wash over you,
as if rain is flooding
our deeply uncut and complete lives.

But as we stand
in the blinding light
of the beautiful sun,
smelling the dried dirt and grass,
we feel the weight of this plate
against our chest.
We feel the weight
of our ancestors' choices
and words
that led up to
this
exact
moment.
Smiling with joy
and exhilaration,
smiling to say,
this is me,
this is us.
My people are still here.

The Rainbow Within the Storm by Autumn (age 15)

Why must people feel the need
to express unnecessary judgement?
We are here on this planet
to love and live.
No,
I do not care
if that person was born a man.
No,
I do not care
if those two guys are holding hands.
Negative comments eat at people's brains
like a worm inside an apple.
Those words rattle in their head
and you can never see it through their eyes,
quiet,
out of panic and fear.
You see this stranger
and you are so quick to judge them.
These people,
who did not choose their path,
feel shackled up
by your rude remarks
and dirty looks.
And for the people who take these hits
and breathe in the fire:
Although our flesh may be weak,
you must keep your spirits strong.
You need to find a way
to continue to stand tall.
Walk on this planet
with pride and grace,
Do not let the storm
get into your tired eyes.
Because without the storm,
there would be no rainbow.

Survivor by Karen "Jazhubi" Salgado (age 15)

I am Jazhubi Salgado.
I am a sexual assault survivor.
I am viewed as an object
to the male community.
I am in control of my own body.
I do not need a man
to tell me who I am
or what I should do with my body.
My body,
my choice.
I am a 15-year-old girl
with a woman's body.
That does not give you the right
to catcall me,
slut-shame me,
or touch me with your filthy hands.
I am smarter,
stronger,
and better than these little boys.
Why is it okay for them
to put their dirty hands
on an eight-year-old?
Why is it okay
for them to be distracted
by my shoulders
if they are showing?
Better yet,
why did my hello kitty pjs attract you?
What made you feel the need to touch me?
I am a 15-year-old,
in an eight-year-old mindset.
They say that you are stuck
at the age of your trauma.
I am ashamed
of letting you make me feel guilty
for what you were doing to me.
I am not okay
with you thinking you have rights

or control over me
and my body.
I should be able to dress however I want
without creepy men looking at me.
I am tired of feeling
like I am powerless
in this society.
I have a voice
and I should be heard.
We should be heard.
No means No!

Little Did She Know by Rosalyn Leyba (age 15)

She never really knew
what she was.
Well,
she did.
She was just a girl.

She had only heard her family
mention the word "Navajo"
a couple times.
From time to time,
she would go into her grandma's room
and see pieces of turquoise
and beaded jewelry.
She thought to herself,
"No one wants to see that.
Where is the gold and silver?"

Family gatherings included telling stories
about her ancestors
and the great history of her people.
All she could focus on
was how painfully hot
and pointless
the whole thing had been.

Slowly and slowly over time,
she was unconsciously assimilating.
All those who came before her,
fought for her,
meant nothing.
Just like pencil on paper,
they could so easily be erased.

She thought to herself,
"But I do not want to go to powwows.
They are so boring.
I do not like the way they sing.
It is so annoying."

Little did she know
that turquoise jewelry she saw
WAS gold.

Little did she know
that all that beaded jewelry she saw
had nothing
but pure love
and prayer
put into them.

Little did she know
those family reunions
she was forced to go to,
told the resilient stories
of her ancestors.

Little did she know
EVERY single powwow
she was forced to go to
was connecting her spiritually
to her ancestors.

Little did she know
every time she heard that stick
hit the drum
it healed her
little by little.

Healed Us.

LITTLE DID SHE KNOW.

The Path by Jeremiah Espinoza (age 16)

I come from a place
considered so rough,
from houses to motels,
from cells to cuffs.
I am now on a journey,
determined to sail,
with no fear of regret
and no fear to fail.
I am grinding like workers
with hammers and nails.
A path through the mountains,
I follow the trail.
The world is in my hands
with God by my side,
with no fear of failure
in any task that I try.
To the top of the mountain,
there is no passing me by.
Like an eagle
I fly,
with my goals
on my mind.

Focused by Jeremiah Espinoza (age 16)

I am a person
with determination and will.
I walk into the fire,
a flame like a grill.
I am unmoved by the wind,
no air from a mill.
I stay committed to goals,
keeping focus on my grind.
I stay patient
my eyes
and my mind
like a line.
Like a laser,
I am aiming.
I am on a roll
to hit my goals
like a paper-route.
The sky starts raining.
My mind,
body,
and soul,
everything is what I am training.
I always keep calm,
I am not a stressor.
I handle my business,
grab a tie from the dresser.
I sail like pirates,
looking for treasure.

Times Up by Brylynn Hurtado (age 17)

Okay class,
you will have 30 minutes.
You may begin.
As I scribble in bubbles
blindly down the line,
I hear others doing the same,
as number 2 pencils
caress the once freshly white paper.
My sheet now bleeds lead
and just like this quiz,
hearty with bubbles.
They say,
"Son,
whew,
you are a piece of work."
Now,
his body must bleed red.
As I get my exam results back,
I blankly look at the teacher,
confused.
She is
unamused
with what I have to say next.
"But Ms.,
you did not teach me
any of this."
Those words go in one ear
and out the other,
just like the bullet
that went through
that young man's body.
Now his insides
color the sidewalk,
the same sidewalk
we once walked down,
skipping each crack
because it was forbidden.
We wanted to keep our mothers' backs

intact.
It was the same sidewalk
the chalk washed off of
when it rained.
As years go on,
that same rain
are the tears
of broken students
who failed another test.
"You can retake it."
But the ironic thing is
you do not get second chances
at life.
As young,
innocent laughter fades
and those same hands
we created arts and crafts with
are in chains
because they outgrew
childish ways.
What they did learn
was to hustle
and make a way,
as the bodies
of their brothers
and sisters
decay.
I speak up again,
one more time,
in a different tone,
with more backbone.
"I am tired
of learning
about the Boston tea party
and the Pythagorean theorem."
If you were not in such a hurry,
you would notice
the mothers worrying
or the protestors scurrying
because they do not want to get caught

at the wrong place
and the wrong time.
Because class,
your life,
I mean exam time
is up.

Golden Butterfly by Yumna Ali (age 17)

We are all like a golden butterfly,
fluttering our ornate wings to wherever life takes us.

At times, we might struggle to fly against the breeze of the wind,
thinking that we cannot endure the journey ahead of us.

But the test of life is miraculous:
It brings hope and perseverance.

That is why the butterfly effect
plays such a prodigious essence.

Because as humans, we underestimate the flutter of our intricate wings.
For the endurance life brings, makes all our efforts worth it.

Let Your Life Speak by Cydney Brown (age 18)

If your eyes have been closed this whole time,
I insist you open them now
to:
the nightmare news,
the black vs. blue,
the white vs. black,
people fighting back,
the unjust trials,
the denials
and the dead man's living smile.
If you have been sleeping
while others have been getting shot,
criticized,
forgotten,
and overlooked,
wake up and look around.
You are not the only inhabitant
of this land.
Stop being meek and truly explore
the power you store
inside you!
You control the future
Stop *start snapping*
snapping to the beat
of society's drum.
They have you numb.
You do not remember
what happiness feels like.
Listen to your life.
When others are spewing hate and bigotry,
find your light.
Do not let life pass you by.
Try to steer clear of obstacles
on this road.
They will set you back.
They know
that you behold
greatness,

so never go slow.
Put your foot on the gas pedal
and Go-Go-Go.
Follow your dreams.
Witness your life
calling out to you
with purpose.
They are purposely planting weeds
in our communities
so we cannot see that we are roses
that can break through concrete.
Do not pick up a gun
because that gun will not set you free.
You are not the only one
trying to escape this reality,
where it feels like no one cares.
You need to speak up now
because your voice
is what the world needs to hear.
And yes,
there will be battles
and fear along the way
because people are afraid
of what they do not understand
and scared of coming together,
standing hand in hand.
But you can demand justice.
Stop!
Breathe *take a deep breath*
and listen to what your life
has to say
before it is too late,
and this world
tries to take everything
you ever loved
away.
Your purpose
can pave the way.

Black Girl by Cydney Brown (age 18)

Black girl walks into a room.
Without even speaking,
people already assume
the tone of her voice,
the place where she lives
the loves that she has lost.
But Black girl does not give a ....
about it.
Black girl lives her life
out loud,
so proud
of her circle of friends
and the journey she is on.
Black girl grew up
not really knowing who she was.
Black girl never really saw her complexion
on TV
and the only thing she knew
about Black history
was that white people
felt guilty.
During all the conversations
about slaves,
they always seemed to look at her
and apologize.
The only Black girl in the room.
It is hard to be yourself
when everyone
is programmed
to put you down.
Look around,
who have you judged,
before you even had a conversation
with them?
If I do not like you,
know that I took the time
to evaluate your character
before I subtracted myself

out of your equation.
And no,
life is not a math problem,
though I am always trying
to find the answers.
Black girl feels like
she is constantly being told
she is not good enough.
In this race,
trying 10x harder
just gets her to the starting line,
while others
have already finished the race.
Question:
when you finish the race,
do you ever look back?
That is where she is.
Black girl just started
her self-love journey.
She has been taught self-hate,
in a PWI since third grade,
where her hair
was the best petting zoo
in the school.
She had to make sure
that no one saw her
as a fool.
She felt like
she had the weight of a million
on her shoulders.
She carried rocks,
those rocks turned into boulders,
and Black girl could not do it anymore:
could not stand the disrespect,
could not stand the lack of representation,
could not stand carrying their guilt too,
could not stand every word she said
being seen as a threat.
And when she spoke,
she could see

how people took a step back,
afraid that Black girl
was going CLAP BACK,
afraid that Black girl
was going CRACK,
afraid that Black girl
was going SMACK
somebody
in the face.
Well,
Black girl is tired
of being misused.
Black girl is not a monster.
You should not be afraid.
Black girl is not a dinner plate
you can eat
when you are hungry.
Black girl is not a pillow
you can cry all your tears into
and make her feel sorry
for your mistakes as well.
Black girl is not loud.
You just never listened before.
Black girl is powerful.
I am powerful.
I am Black girl.

Unknown by Amari (age 18)

We can be invisible in their eyes,
who have not seen
or heard
the pain
that was carried from
and for
our parents.
We are the people
from all four directions
north,
south,
west,
and east.
Words strain
from the minds of the innocent.
All this pain
cannot fit into a frame,
unless you have one
that is strong enough for survivors.
Our frame
is community and unity.
They blame us
for our anger and rage
but never look in the books.
The knowledge is alive.
Mother earth is our teacher.
How are we giving her
what she needs?
It is fatal
to keep her
from breathing
because all flourishing
is mutual.

Mirrors by Amari (age 18)

Red
is the representation
of life,
war,
anger,
courage,
and love.
Only you decide
what this color
means to you.

You are as human
as me.
I was given this beyond feeling,
she,
her,
he,
him,
they,
them.
Sun mothering my skin,
the hair of my stories will live on.
But,
I sometimes wonder
if my body
is ever going to see the next day.
I relive my lives
before this one
and see my present.
It is funny:
some sayings are true,
so why can't everything be true?
Covered up with sweet dinner lies
and "oh no, no it was an accident,
I was just defending myself."
Only the right people are looking
but she was on the news
because of green and flesh.

Am I not as important?
I am human
and a woman too.
This world was designed for me
to have a baby daddy
who is cruel to me
and my child.
Keys are locked in between my fingers
before I get to my car.

Red
is the representation
of life,
war,
anger,
courage,
and love.
Only you decide
what this color means to you.

I speak what I see
and I see a whole lot of bosh.
We,
as people,
see people
and never have empathy
for the face behind the dirt,
so caught up in the fast.
The city is the fast life,
with my days mixed
into a whole lifetime.
I can never unsee you.

I keep up with myself
and the world
that does not care
if I die tomorrow,
unless I had thousands of cameras
pointing at me.
Strangers would know

before my mother.
Blood is in the eyes
of your enemy
but never in yours.
Why is that?
So many unanswered questions
that never seem to have answers.

I was not made for this world
but I still exist.
It is still power for the people.
Resilience will always run red
through our veins.

Red
is the representation
of life,
war,
anger,
courage,
and love.
Only you decide
what this color means to you.

The Universe Took Its Time With You by Aakanksha Adya (age 18)

I like to believe
that you were born
because the universe
has faith in you
and what you will do.

You bring something
immeasurable
to this universe.

It has carved out
a little piece of fate
to place
in your innocent hands
to protect
and pursue.

Pro Black by Tracie Taylor (age 21)

I am tired of my people
struggling,
young Black men
hustlin'
on the streets,
seven days a week.
I sit back
and I think:
They say the youth
are our future
but we are losing our youth.
Sorry,
but I must admit
my truth.
We are killing one another.
We are both black.
Why not be like brothers?
I am sick of seeing mothers
bury their sons,
sick of seeing
Black boys pick up a gun.
They are already being told
that they are another statistic
and they belong in prison
or in a grave.
I am sure
this is not
what the slaves died for.
Stop being institutionalized
and you will realize:
We are stronger than we think.
Come on now Black people,
think.

I Choose to Rise by Evelyn Neal (age 21)

I choose to rise
because I am an African American woman
in a world that judges you
the moment you are born.
Art saved my life.
Poetry brings meaning to the word survival
that I had to endure as a child.

I rise
because the color of my skin
brought meaning to my life.
My dark complexion
is not a threat
but a beauty of melanin sunshine.
My eyes are strong
and courageous
for capturing the traumatic wicked moments
of hate and pain
in this world
we call freedom.

I rise to define my survival.
I am feared by the color of my skin
but I accept that I am strong and moral by nature.
My ability to keep moving with life's current rhythms
and continue to survive
despite the disregard for my existence
means I am truly extraordinary.

I can SHOUT and run wild
defining the odds
that those who seek pain and anger upon me
will never hurt
nor spite me
because I will rise.

I am a survivor.
As a 21 year-old,

life has taught me
to defy the odds of depression,
anxiety,
stress,
suicide,
sexual and physical abuse.

All because I stood strong
and beat the odds
of life or death.

Dear Black Men by Evelyn Neal (age 21)

Dear Black Men,
Your skin is so gentle but rich and pure.
Your features define your strength,
your purpose,
your survival.
I see you.
I value you.
I cherish you.
As a black woman,
your presence matters.
As a black woman,
I acknowledge you as my brother,
father,
friend,
uncle,
nephew,
son,
husband,
and protector.
Do not be afraid
for you are not alone.
They target you because of your potential.
You are feared
but strong and moral by nature.
Our communication has been interrupted
by the sounds of gunshots,
imprisonment,
poverty,
and lack of prayers.
Your ability to keep moving with life's current rhythms
and continue to survive
despite the disregard for your existence
means you are truly extraordinary.
Please see me standing in the front line
fighting for you,
with you.
Dear Black Men,
I Love You.

Made in the USA
Middletown, DE
24 February 2023

25509682R00046